DRAW 50
DOGS

DRAW 50
DOGS

LEE J. AMES

Kingfisher Books

Kingfisher Books, Grisewood & Dempsey Limited,
Elsley House, 24–30 Great Titchfield Street,
London W1P 7AD

First published in Great Britain in 1990
by Kingfisher Books
Published by arrangement with Doubleday,
a division of Bantam Doubleday Dell Publishing Group, Inc.

BRITISH LIBRARY CATALOGUING IN PUBLICATION DATA
Ames, Lee J.
   Draw 50 dogs.
   1. Drawings. Special subjects: Dogs. Techniques – For
   children.
   I. Title
   743'.6974442
ISBN 0 86272 437 6

Phototypeset by Southern Positives and Negatives (SPAN),
Lingfield, Surrey
Printed in Spain

To Butchie Dell Ames, Le May's Red Whattis (Tiny),
and Sam (Née Restless)

And thanks again to Holly Moylan, super-helper

TO THE READER

This book will show you a way to draw dogs. You need not start with the first illustration. Choose whichever you wish. When you have chosen, follow the step-by-step method shown. *Very lightly* and *carefully*, sketch out step number one. However, this step, which is the easiest, should be done most carefully. Step number two is added on top of step number one, also lightly and also very carefully. Step number three is sketched right on top of numbers one and two. Continue in this way to the last step.

It may seem strange to ask you to be extra careful when you are drawing what seem to be the easiest first steps, but this is most important because a careless mistake at the beginning may spoil the whole picture at the end. As you sketch out each step, watch the spaces between the lines, as well as the lines themselves, and see that they are the same. After each step, you may want to lighten your work by pressing it with a plastic, or 'putty' rubber (available at art supply shops).

When you have finished, you may want to redo the final step in India ink with a fine brush or pen – or use a fine pointed felt-tip pen. When the ink is dry, use the plastic rubber to clean off the pencil lines. The rubber will not affect the ink.

Continued over page

Here are some suggestions: In the first few steps, even when all seems quite correct, you might do well to hold your work up to a mirror. Sometimes the mirror shows that you've twisted the drawing off to one side without being aware of it. At first you may find it difficult to draw the egg shapes or circles, or just to make the pencil go where you want it to. Don't be discouraged. The more you practise, the more you will develop control. Use a compass to help you if you wish; professional artists do!

The only equipment you will need will be a medium or soft pencil, paper, the plastic rubber and, if you wish, a compass, pen or brush and India ink – or a felt-tip pen. The first steps in this book are shown darker than necessary so that they can be clearly seen. (Keep your work very light.)

Remember, this book presents only one method of drawing. In a most enjoyable way, it will help you to develop a certain skill and control. But there are many other ways of drawing to which you can apply this skill, and the more of them you try, the more interesting your drawings will be.

Lee J. Ames

TO THE PARENT OR TEACHER

Drawing, like any other skill, requires practice and discipline. But this does not mean that rewards cannot be found along every step of the way.

While contemporary methods of art instruction rightly emphasize freedom of expression and experimentation, they often lose sight of a very basic, traditional and valuable approach: the 'follow me, step-by-step' way that I learned as a youth.

Just as a beginning musician is given simple, beautiful melodies to play, so too the young artist needs to gain a sense of satisfaction and pride in his or her work as soon as possible. The 'do as I do' steps that I have laid out here provide the opportunity to mimic finished images, images the young artist is eager to draw.

Mimicry is prerequisite for developing creativity. We learn the use of our tools through mimicry, and once we have those tools we are free to express ourselves in whatever fashion we choose. The use of this book will help lay a solid foundation for the child, one that can be continued with other books in the *Draw 50* series, or even used to complement different approaches to drawing.

Above all, the joy of making a credible, attractive image will encourage the child to continue and grow as an artist, giving him even more of a sense of pride and accomplishment when his friends say, "Peter can draw a dog better than anyone else!"

Lee J. Ames

Have fun with
your drawings . . .

THE HOUND BREEDS
Afghan Hound

Basenji

Basset Hound

Beagle

Black and Tan Coonhound

Bloodhound

Borzoi

Dachshund

Greyhound

Irish Wolfhound

THE TERRIERS
Airedale Terrier

Bedlington Terrier

Bull Terrier

Cairn Terrier

Dandie Dinmont Terrier

Fox Terrier (Wire)

Kerry Blue Terrier

Scottish Terrier

Sealyham Terrier

West Highland White Terrier

THE WORKING BREEDS
Alaskan Malamute

Boxer

Collie (Rough)

Doberman Pinscher

German Shepherd Dog

Great Dane

Mastiff

Old English Sheepdog

Pembroke Welsh Corgi

St. Bernard

Samoyed

Shetland Sheepdog

Standard Schnauzer

THE SPORTING BREEDS
Cocker Spaniel

English Setter

Golden Retriever

Irish Setter

Pointer

Weimaraner

THE NON-SPORTING BREEDS
Bichon Frisé

Boston Terrier

Bulldog

Chow Chow

Dalmatian

Lhasa Apso

Standard Poodle

THE TOY BREEDS
Chihuahua

Pomeranian

Pug

Yorkshire Terrier

ABOUT THE AUTHOR

Lee J. Ames has been earning his living as an artist for almost forty years. He began his career working on Walt Disney's *Fantasia* and *Pinocchio*. He has taught at the School of Visual Arts in New York City and, more recently, at Dowling College on Long Island, New York State. He was, for a time, director of his own advertising agency and illustrator for several magazines. Mr Ames has illustrated over one hundred books, from preschool picture books to postgraduate texts. When not working, he battles on the tennis court. A native New Yorker, Lee J. Ames lives in Dix Hills, Long Island, with his wife, Jocelyn, their three dogs, and a calico cat.